I Want to Talk With
my TEEN About

MONEY
MANAGEMENT

BY
LISA CRAYTON

Standard®
PUBLISHING
Bringing The Word to Life

Cincinnati, Ohio

Credits

I Want to Teach My Child About Money
Management
© 2006 Standard Publishing, Cincinnati,
Ohio. A division of Standex International
Corporation. All rights reserved. Printed
in China.

Credits
Produced by Susan Lingo Books™
Cover by Diana Walters

13 12 11 10 09 08 07 06   9 8 7 6 5 4 3 2 1
0-7847-1897-0

Contents

Introduction

Why teach your teen about money management?

In recent years, teens have consistently scored poorly on money surveys designed to test basic knowledge about money matters. Realizing the seriousness of the matter, educators, financial institutions, and even the federal government have stepped up efforts to increase teens' understanding of money matters. And they all agree that parents *need* to be involved in equipping their teens to manage money well. Teens on the brink of adulthood need to know basic financial principles, how to apply them to life, and how to make wise decisions to avoid excessive debt, bankruptcy, and other financial dilemmas.

In the pages of *I Want to Talk With My Teens About Money Management,* you'll discover encouragement, inspiration, and informative tips for parents of teens 13 to 19 who are seeking help in teaching their teens concepts that will shape wise spending and saving decisions for today and for future goals such as college, employment, and more.

Teaching your teen about money management and how God helps us handle finances will prepare him or her to handle the rigors of managing money while working part-time in high school, attending college, and landing a first career job. Train up your teens in the way God wants them to go, and years from now they'll be thankful for the great foundation you've prepared!

Lisa Crayton

Where Do You Stand?

Working toward helping your teen learn about money management and how it affects his life is a valuable life skill! The following questionnaire will help you evaluate your own strengths and weaknesses with money management and where your own philosophies fit in. Circle the box with the number that best corresponds to your answer. Then add the total of your answers and check out the How You Scored box! (Retake the quiz after reading the book to see if your score changed!)

OPTIONS

❶ Strongly agree

❷ Agree somewhat

❸ Disagree somewhat

❹ Strongly disagree

I UNDERSTAND MONEY HAS NO VALUE BY ITSELF; IT'S SIMPLY A MEANS OF TRADING.

❶ ❷ ❸ ❹

I SET ASIDE TIME TO TALK WITH MY TEEN ABOUT MONEY AND HOW WE USE IT.

❶ ❷ ❸ ❹

I VIEW MONEY AS SIMPLY A TOOL TO HELP ME ACHIEVE GOALS.

❶ ❷ ❸ ❹

I'VE DEVELOPED A BUDGET, HAVE WRITTEN IT ON PAPER, AND STICK TO IT FAITHFULLY.

❶ ❷ ❸ ❹

I WATCH MY SPENDING AND DON'T WASTE MONEY ON THINGS I DON'T TRULY NEED.

❶ ❷ ❸ ❹

I WORK TO SET, ASSESS, OR IMPROVE MY FINANCIAL GOALS REGULARLY.

❶ ❷ ❸ ❹

I SAVE REGULARLY AND CONSISTENTLY IN A SAVINGS OR INVESTMENT ACCOUNT.

❶ ❷ ❸ ❹

I HAVE A WELL THOUGHT OUT PLAN FOR FUTURE GOALS OR RETIREMENT.

❶ ❷ ❸ ❹

I MAKE IT A POINT TO DONATE A PORTION OF WHAT I EARN TO HELP SOMEONE IN NEED.

❶ ❷ ❸ ❹

I WOULDN'T SAY THAT MONEY IS THE MOST IMPORTANT THING IN LIFE.

❶ ❷ ❸ ❹

HOW YOU SCORED

10—20 Give yourself a pat on the back! You're able to plan ahead, commit to your goals, and move ahead without overspending or undersaving. The habits you've worked so hard to adopt are the ones you want to instill in your teen and will serve him well throughout his life!

21—31 Your money skills might need polishing to really shine! You're a moderate spender—but also a moderate saver. Though you probably have a budget, it may not be written down or stuck to like glue. Help your teen realize that careful spending and saving are important all the time.

32—40 Money may travel a little too quickly through your fingers! Though you probably realize money doesn't hold all of life's answers, you tend to see it as a way of getting what you want immediately instead of waiting until you can afford it. With a little budget control and a bit of willpower, you'll be back on the path to healthy money management.

Money in Perspective

By the time kids become teens, they've had experience handling money—but may not know how to do it wisely. Many teens exhibit attitudes and behaviors that undermine effective money management. If we teach the proper ways to use and manage money, these positive lessons will last our teens a lifetime.

Money is simply a tool of trade.

Teens need to know that, for all its buying power, money is simply a tool. It is neither good nor bad, and it does not have a body, soul, or spirit. The tool becomes operative when we put it to work through spending, saving, or investing. Sharing this basic money principle brings much-needed biblical balance to media messages that associate money with glamour, love, and success.

Money has no real value of its own.

key point
MONEY IS AN INANIMATE TOOL TO USE.

Used throughout the world, money has evolved as the primary medium of exchange, replacing bartering. But when we come right down to it, money is just paper and metal. It's only as valuable as what it can buy, and in varying countries that purchasing power easily fluctuates. For example, $50 in American money will not buy the same amount of food at a restaurant in Tokyo, Paris, or London. That's because the dollar's value is different in each country.

Without a doubt, money is a necessity of life. It is quite handy, enabling us to trade it for desired goods and services. Without it, we couldn't go to movies or doctors, and a trip to the mall or arcade would be useless! That easy-to-grasp concept resonates with teens used to spending for comic books, CDs, hand-held games, clothing, and other possessions.

key point
EVERY TOOL HAS A PURPOSE—SO DOES MONEY!

Different countries use different items for money, but coins and bills are still the most common. Gone are the days when salt, feathers, leaves, and other items were commonly used for money. But even today in one area of the Pacific Ocean, large stones are used for some transactions. Some of these stones weigh as much as 500 pounds! Not handy pocket change! Help your teen see how the dollar stacks up internationally by surfing over to one of the online currency conversion websites such as www.xe.com/ucc.

MIDDLE-SCHOOL MEMOS

Play a money board game like Monopoly with your teen. After the game, discuss how some of your teen's decisions were wise or unwise and how the consequences could have been different.

King Solomon was already rich when he began to rule, having been born the son of prosperous King David. But when God asked what he would like most, Solomon didn't blink. He asked for a discerning heart. In other words, he wanted wisdom over wealth. The result? *"The Lord was pleased that Solomon had asked for this"* (1 Kings 3:10). What do you or your teen need right now that could help you more than money?

BIG BIBLE POINT

Read 1 Kings 3:1-14 aloud with your teen, then discuss:

• How does this verse relate to money?

• Why was God pleased with Solomon's desire for wisdom over wealth?

• Do you think the fact that Solomon already had wealth made it easier for him not to want more? Why?

People assign value to money.

One man's treasure is another man's trash!

This familiar adage may have run through your mind too many times to count when looking at the quality, color, or size of other people's possessions. If nothing else, it proves that value is in the eye of the beholder.

key point
PEOPLE ASSIGN VALUE TO ITEMS AND SERVICES.

People assign value to money. Whether its pounds, yen, pesos, or dollars, someone had to purposely assign the value of each in order for it to be used as a medium of exchange. Assigning value is similar to putting a price tag on an item in our own minds. Teens need to understand that money has limited value compared to other things in life—especially family, good friends, and, of course, a relationship with God. These are the enduring, priceless possessions that make life richer, happier, and more meaningful. Help your teen understand value by encouraging him to place money in its rightful place in his life.

STOP & CONSIDER

"The tongue of the righteous is choice silver, but the heart of the wicked is of little value" (Proverbs 10:20).

✦ Where does value lie in your life?

✦ Why is an unclean heart like a spoiled treasure?

"That man is richest whose pleasures are cheapest."
— Henry David Thoreau

Proverbs 20:14 tells of a deceitful buyer who questioned the value of a purchase in order to get a better deal. "It's no good!" said the buyer—then he boasted about the purchase. The buyer's duplicity is very similar to that of people who buy clothing, wear it with the tags on, then return it to the store as if never worn. Talk about gross! But other than the hygienic issues involved, this practice is dishonest and devalues how we use our money. Discuss such practices with your teens and stress the importance of avoiding such devaluing behaviors.

Shopping is fun—but use good choices to get the best values!

Top Shopping Influencers

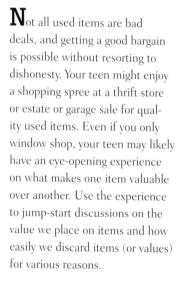

26.7%	**WORD OF MOUTH**
20.3%	**NEWSPAPER ADS**
18.9%	**IN-STORE PROMOTIONS**

(USA Today)

Not all used items are bad deals, and getting a good bargain is possible without resorting to dishonesty. Your teen might enjoy a shopping spree at a thrift store or estate or garage sale for quality used items. Even if you only window shop, your teen may likely have an eye-opening experience on what makes one item valuable over another. Use the experience to jump-start discussions on the value we place on items and how easily we discard items (or values) for various reasons.

Share a virtual shopping trip around the world with your teen. Ask what countries she'd shop in and why (based on the present value of the dollar). Then use the Internet to compare prices and values for various goods and services in several countries.

Money is a tool for building up.

What plans have your family made for the future? Do they include the purchase of a new home, financing your child's college education, or retiring financially comfortable? Time has a way of sneaking up on us. While the time to fulfill your goals may seem far off, you may not have as much time as you think.

key point
MONEY HELPS US REACH OUR GOALS.

REMEMBER...

How you manage your family's finances today will determine whether you have enough money to accomplish your goals.

A stumbling block or a stepping stone? Money can only fulfill one role in our lives. Your teen needs to understand that money can either guide us toward financial independence or detour us into financial ruin. The key is whether we squander it or save and invest it. We should also consider using our money to serve others. That may seem impossible, if your teen is already struggling to remain afloat financially. But consider the widow in Mark 12:41-44. While

she gave less money than the others, Jesus lauded her giving. Why? She gave all she had. She used money as a tool to build and serve!

key point
GREED CAN DESTROY OUR PLANS AND GOALS.

Help your teen see how her money choices affect her today and tomorrow.

Discuss the meaning of the adage "If at first you don't succeed, try, try, again" and how it relates to handling money wisely.

LOOK WHAT YOUR CHARITABLE CHANGE CAN BUY FOR PEOPLE IN NEED!

66¢ buys a disaster-related coloring book

$3.00 buys a comfort kit for one victim

$6.00 buys a blanket for a disaster shelter

$10.00 buys a day of groceries for a family

$20.00 buys a home clean-up kit

(American Red Cross)

Help your teen to build a foundation of heart-felt gifts to others. As you encourage her to tithe and save, also laud her for giving sacrificially to build up and encourage those in need. Recent calamities like Hurricanes Katrina and Rita and the tsunami in Asia prove how needed money is when disaster strikes. What a good example of how money can be used to build up—literally! It is not always the amount that is given that is most important. Teens' seemingly meager offerings, when coupled with other donors' money, will add up—quickly!

Perhaps your teen wants to donate money to build others up but doesn't know where to begin. Encourage your teen to start small by seeking coin donations from family, friends, and neighbors. After coins are collected and rolled, deposit them in the bank and either write a check or money order to the chosen charity. Encourage your teen to enclose a letter from the heart, sharing why and how the donation was made possible.

TAKE 5

* What do my money habits reveal about my faith?
* Is my money management helping or hindering my goals?
* Why must I teach my teen to save for her goals?
* How can I help my teen build strong faith that is a foundation for solid money management?
* What are goals money can help achieve?

Money has perceived power.

Proverbs 22:6 encourages us to "train a child in the way he should go, and when he is old he will not turn from it." We need to help teens understand the influence money has on a person's life—and how to keep it in check.

Money has the power to label people.

What's in a label? Everything—if we believe advertising claims that equate "designer label" products and services with high quality. Like adults, many teens buy into the false notion that a designer label or higher price makes a product better. Generic drugs can

key point

LABELS ARE NOT ALWAYS ACCURATE.

be as beneficial as name-brand prescription medications, and store-brand groceries can be as yummy as company-branded products—and are much more reasonably priced!

Get your teen thinking about the power of labels when it comes to people. Ask:

✦ **How can a good or bad label make someone feel?**

✦ **How can labels become self-fulfilling?**

✦ **Why should labels be avoided in choosing friends?**

Some manufacturers sell similar products under different trade names to reach consumers of varying income brackets. When my son was small, I was surprised to learn the company that sold my favorite disposable diapers also sold another brand for $3 less. I quickly switched to that brand, saving a significant amount of money each month. More recently, a friend reminded me that some companies manufacture their products under different names for varying reasons.

> **key point**
> MONEY HAS "POWER" TO LABEL PEOPLE.

Like labels on food, assigning labels to people may not be accurate descriptions of true worth. Yet society continues to label people based many things, including money: poor, middle-class, or rich; white collar or blue collar; working class or elite. Teens need to realize that God does not afford a better, cushier place in his heart or in heaven for people based on money.

Money may have earthly power, but not heavenly sway! Help your teen grasp this truth by encouraging his or her friendships with people of different economic backgrounds.

10 LABEL-DEFINING FACTORS

- YOUR TYPE OF JOB OR CAREER
- YOUR JOB TITLE
- YOUR INCOME
- THE TYPE OF CAR YOU DRIVE
- YOUR HOUSE OR WHERE YOU LIVE
- YOUR WEIGHT
- YOUR HEIGHT
- YOUR RACE OR ETHNICITY
- HOW YOU DRESS
- YOUR RELIGIOUS BELIEFS

Some people refuse to buy products that do not bear well-known labels. If you associate labels with power, status, and popularity, you've no doubt transferred those beliefs to your teen. Honestly assess your habits, asking God to help you to get beyond the allure—and false power—of labels and money.

> **Read Acts 10:34** with your teen. Discuss how the verse relates to money and finances. How can this verse help us overcome the use of labels and the way labels affect us through money?

Money has purchasing power.

Have you ever heard it said that "money makes the world go 'round"? Of course we know that's not so! But money does afford us purchasing power. Our money is *our* money; as long as we don't do anything illegal with it, we can spend it almost any way we choose. It's important for teens to know that purchasing power should not add up to irresponsibility.

Spending money without thought of personal, family, or household needs (rather than wants) strains relationships and leads to financial instability.

key point
MONEY IS A LIMITED RESOURCE.

key point
USE AND SPEND MONEY RESPONSIBLY!

Remind your teen that money has the power to help—or hurt—us.

It is a well-known fact that many people are just a paycheck or two from financial ruin. Often it's not because they don't earn enough money but because their financial obligations consume almost 100 percent of all they make. A crisp $20 bill holds a lot of promise—and power—for a teen with a foot-long wish list! To her, money may have the power to answer life's problems. It's important to teach her the real truth about money, about its perceived power, and about spending responsibly! Remember: *The purchasing power of money is a privilege!*

For most teens, money holds power, promise—and problems!

CONSIDER THIS...

CONSIDER THIS... Teens need access to their own money to make a connection with it. Providing your young teen with money for routine or special purchases helps him learn about handling money thoughtfully and responsibly.

We've all known teens who blow their entire allowance or paycheck the day they receive it. Some parents chalk it up to "kids being kids." Wrong. If your teen son or daughter doesn't learn how to control spending now, it will be more difficult later in life. Consider talking to your teen about his spending and savings habits. Brainstorm possibilities that will inspire him to spend less and save more.

Teens need to know that purchasing power is increased when they get more for less. Encouraging the use of cents-off coupons or shopping during sales can help your teen see how much further money can go. Teens may especially appreciate coupons for discounted movie matinees, fast food, or two-for-one meal specials. Find them in your newspapers or mail to increase purchasing power!

CHECK IT OUT!

Go to www.valpak. com to find coupons that teens will find helpful in stretching their bucks and budgets!

WHAT POWER DOES MONEY HAVE OVER YOU?
(Score one point for each true answer.)

1. You live for payday or allowance day.
2. You often dream about what you want to buy.
3. You can't seem to make money last for long.
4. You rarely have money left to save or donate.
5. You don't keep close track of your spending.
6. Having lots of money makes you feel good.
7. Money seems to control what you do each day.

If your score is more than 5, you're giving money great power in your life! Remember that money is a tool to help accomplish goals and only has the power we assign it.

Money has power for financial freedom.

When we use our money wisely, we establish a secure financial future for ourselves and our loved ones. Our money works smarter, not harder, when we budget for routine monthly expenses, including utilities, groceries, mortgage or rent. Help your teen realize that budgeting money makes sense. Instead of scrambling to pay for needs and wants, make sure you have the money *before* you need it. Your budget should take into account seasonal items such as back-to-school clothes, holiday shopping, and family birthdays and celebrations.

key point

"BUDGET" IS NOT A DIRTY WORD.

> **Money** *cannot* **purchase** *what the* **heart** *desires.*
> —Chinese proverb

Discuss this proverb with your teen and how it applies to the power of faith over money!

Take the mystery out of budgeting for your teen in four easy steps. (1) *Keep it simple.* Use the easiest system for you, whether it's a notebook or computer-based spreadsheet. (2) *Be realistic.* Your budget should reflect items your teen feels are important—even if you might consider those items non-essentials. (3) *Get help.* If budgeting proves not to be your forte or your teen's, consider having your spouse or a financial professional help with tailoring a budget. (4) *Don't give up.* At first, a budget may seem like a strait jacket to your teen, but encourage him to stick with it. Assure him that over time it will get easier—and is so worth it!

Remind your teen that expecting the unexpected is important and that he needs to set money aside for emergencies such as car repairs or unexpected medical care. Discuss with your teen how she can make sure emergency situations don't impact her finances. Remind your teen that, just as good money management provides financial freedom, poor planning can keep us strapped—and trapped!

BIG BIBLE POINT

Read aloud Matthew 6:25-31 with your teen. Then discuss these questions:

• How do these verses relate to the value you place on money as personal security?

• If we're not to worry about tomorrow, why save or invest?

• How can fear undermine our security?

There's *negative* power in money when bankruptcy or crippling debt looms!

Consumer bankruptcy is at an all-time high, with one in seventy-two households filing for bankruptcy in 2004. Filing for bankruptcy can severely hinder your ability to buy a home or car or to obtain future credit. Help your teen know that bankruptcy is not an easy out and has serious consequences for future financial freedom.

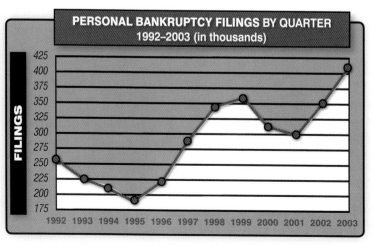

PERSONAL BANKRUPTCY FILINGS BY QUARTER
1992–2003 (in thousands)

FILINGS

425
400
375
350
325
300
275
250
225
200
175

1992 1993 1994 1995 1996 1997 1998 1999 2000 2001 2002 2003

Money has only the power we allow it to have.

Remember the TV show *Who Wants to Be a Millionaire?* Its rapid rise in popularity proved that many people answered the question in the title with a resounding "Me!" Many people really believe having more money will cure most, if not all, of their problems. But sometimes the more money you have the greater your problems. As it has been said, "Money magnifies what you already are." In other words, more money won't make you a better budgeter, wiser spender, or consistent giver.

key point
MAKE MONEY SERVE YOU!

Share the story of Ananias and Sapphira in Acts 5:1-10 with your teen. Then discuss how money affected both of their lives by revealing their true characters.

key point
SERVE GOD— NOT MONEY.

It is important for your teen to realize that we choose the role money plays in our life but that some things about money are better "caught" than taught. When parents consistently handle money in a way that honors God, it makes a lasting impact on their teens. Restraining money's influence in our lives is the real message behind Mathew 6:24. When we help our teens understand the importance of not serving money or treating it as our master, we help them avoid destructive spending patterns and behaviors.

BIG BIBLE POINT

Read Matthew 6:24 with your teen, then discuss these questions:

• How can money become like a powerful master?

• Why is it not wise to give money too much power in our lives?

• How can we use money to serve our one true master — God?

SOMEONE IS WATCHING YOU!
Teens need to understand that
spending habits aren't secret —
credit reports are real!

Unmanageable credit-card debt, gambling, and frequent loans from family and friends are signs that money has a stranglehold on a person's life. Gambling especially has become a major money issue for teens, due in large part to the increased number of Internet gaming sites. Talk honestly with your teen about the dangers of gambling. Identify common forms of gambling such as buying scratch cards and playing the lottery and why they should be avoided.

Discuss the purpose and use of credit reports. Consumers are allowed to receive one free credit report a year from the three major credit-reporting bureaus:

- Equifax® (www.Equifax.com)
- Experian® (www.experian.com)
- TransUnion® (www.transunion.com)

When you don't have a lot of disposable income, money may seem like a ticket to heaven. Help your teen appreciate the good and free blessings in her life. Encourage her to make a list, write a poem or song, or even prepare a skit that focuses on everyday blessings. Encourage her to share her ideas with you. If your teen has a tough time with this, try to discern what really is bothering her, since depression often sparks overspending.

NEARLY 8 IN 10 CREDIT REPORTS CONTAIN ERRORS.

Money is not to be worshiped.

Using a faulty compass could easily point you to an unplanned destination. Worshiping money has a similar effect. Help your teen stay on track, consistently resisting the temptation to allow money to rule him, and assure him that God alone is to be our object of worship and praise.

Money can enslave us.

key point

GOD IS OUR ONE TRUE MASTER.

The idea of bowing down to a piggy bank, wallet, or bank vault seems ludicrous—but a worshipful attitude toward money is not that unusual. Teens need to realize that money should never have more prominence than our Creator! God is the only true Master we're to serve. Help your teen understand this by placing a high priority on personal and family devotions without limitations, by pursuing meaningful employment and career goals without being consumed by wealth acquisition, and by tithing and giving without grumbling.

key point

DON'T BOW DOWN TO MONEY.

Teens who can't wait to get their hands on more money than "mere" allowance may not grasp the seriousness of being enslaved by money. Remind your teen that even Jesus had to face, and overcome, the allure of fame and fortune. Satan offered Jesus "all the kingdoms of the world and their splendor" (Matthew 4:9). But Jesus resisted the temptation of untold wealth through God's Word. Memorizing Scripture is a great way to remind your teen we're to worship only God!

DEBT CREATES WORRY AND STRESS EVEN IN TEENS.

Ever had the wind blow a dollar bill out of your hand? Such an occurrence brings to mind Proverbs 23:5: "Cast but a glance at riches, and they are gone, for they will surely sprout wings and fly off to the sky like an eagle." Can you remember times when your money seemed to fly away quicker than you could earn it? What can you teach your teen about the transitory nature of money—and where true wealth lies?

From a recent survey of gamblers…

43% LOST MORE THAN THEY WON

33% CAME OUT EVEN

20% WON MORE THAN THEY LOST

TRY THESE!

Compulsive spending can often be tamed by the "24-hour rule." Encourage your teen to wait a day before purchasing anything that suddenly seems like a must-have. By consistently following the 24-hour rule, you can teach your teen how to avoid the compulsive spending trap.

Famous people often struggle with their fortunes. Have your teen choose a favorite star and find out how he or she made or lost wealth. Discuss ways your teen can avoid such pitfalls if suddenly thrust into the limelight due to a scholastic, athletic, or heroic achievement.

Read Matthew 6:24-34 and discuss the differences between earthly riches and true wealth.

People waste money through compulsive spending, gambling, and other bad habits. According to 1 Timothy 6:10, when these habits are based on a love of money, sorrow is inevitable. Take an active role in helping your teen understand that money, when it becomes one's master, can enslave and bring sorrow rather than empowerment and happiness. Encourage your son or daughter to handle money wisely—not worshipfully.

Money is meant to serve us—not vice versa.

Service with a smile! Waiters, tellers, gas attendants, ushers—throughout the week we come in contact with people who serve us in various capacities. How do you feel when you don't receive the kind of service expected? You probably feel angry, frustrated, or cheated. The kind of service we receive can make or break our purchasing experience. For example, we expect a pricey hotel to offer better service and amenities than a budget hotel. We also feel indignant if we don't feel we have received our money's worth. Our service wasn't all it could be!

DID YOU KNOW?

key point
MANAGE MONEY SO IT SERVES YOU!

It's common to tip 15% of your total food bill—even if the service is lousy! Demand more from your money!

One way money serves us is when we get exceptional values. Model your bargain-conscious side often. Encourage your teen to ask if there is an applicable student discount at restaurants, movie theaters, and other favorite locales.

Perhaps the reason that our money management may not be effective at times is because we're not letting our money be all it can be. Money is meant to serve us—not the other way around. Ask your teen what might happen if he ups his service expectations for money. He might not buy the priciest stereo or clothes when an alternative exists. If we expect more from our money, we might save more, think twice before taking out loans, or refrain from maxing out credit cards.

key point

EXPECT MORE FROM YOUR MONEY!

The idea of money serving them may not click with teens, but they can relate to the concept of an animal as a servant. For instance, a guide dog provides a valuable service to visually impaired persons. Challenge your teen to think of ways a pet also provides a service to its owner. A dog may guard and protect its owner and home.

A pet brings pleasure, thus serving by adding joy and fun to the household. Don't stop there. Also discuss the responsibilities that come with owning a pet. Remind your teen that, like owning a pet, money requires responsibility and will serve us well if we take care of it!

Brainstorm ways that money serves us, such as through …

* providing housing
* buying food
* reaching goals
* providing an education
* earning interest
* giving help to others
* providing a car
* giving security
* providing healthcare

"The rich rule over the poor, and the borrower is servant to the lender." What does Proverbs 22:7 teach us about not serving money but letting money serve us?

Does your teen like shopping at one store that carries only one brand? Discuss these reasons to shop around so your money serves you better!

Some stores offer frequent-shopper cards.

Some stores may have a larger variety.

Some stores may offer better discounts.

Prices vary based on location and store size.

Some stores honor competitors' prices.

Similar brands have a similar fit and style.

Some retailers offer coupons or special deals.

Money creates important choices.

All-you-can-eat restaurants are a parent's dream. Our kids can eat as much as they want at very reasonable prices. The choices seem endless! But have you noticed how much food is wasted at such restaurants?

key point
CHOOSE TO USE MONEY WISELY.

Most kids love the thrill of going back and forth to the food bar but really can't eat as much as they take. Even teens have a tough time eating all of their food after the first plate or two. A classic case of their eyes—and choices—being too big for their stomachs!

Look for ways to help your teen see the choices money creates for us—and how our decisions may cost us greatly!

Such outings are lessons in making wise choices, affording ample opportunities to share with teens the importance of making wise choices, especially with money. Turn a great buffet dinner into a teachable moment by helping your teen understand that making good choices is key to financial health just as good food choices are key to physical health.

TRY THIS!

Next time you make out a grocery list, enlist your teen's help. Have him separate and list his "needs" and "wants." Chat about the differences between *needs* and *wants* to emphasize that we have choices when shopping—and when spending our money.

It is a parent's job to provide room for teens to grow into financial responsibility. This won't happen if we don't allow our teens to make money choices—even poor ones. Let your teen decide how to spend her allowance or paycheck from an after-school job. Make it clear that your teen is responsible for good money management as well as poor money decisions. Discuss possible consequences as you guide your teen in her choices. Remind her that every decision has a consequence and that identifying priorities in spending and saving can help with decision making.

TARGET MOMENT

Help your teen understand the two main choices money creates for us: to be in control of our finances or to be slaves of debt.

PARENT POINTER

You're the best role model in teaching your teen how to make good money choices. Do you use money wisely or abuse it? Do you serve God and others with your money?

key point
PRIORITIZE YOUR NEEDS AND WANTS.

Encourage wise choices and financial responsibility. For example, if your teen likes to rent videos from the library or a video rental store, discuss the consequences of late payments. Perhaps one late payment gets a warning, but the privilege of renting videos gets revoked for a time after the second. Keep in mind that your teen won't always have you around to direct choices, so it's best to help him develop a sound foundation from which to consistently make wise choices. Helping your teen understand the consequences of money decisions and not always bailing him out prepares him for the reality of living responsibly on a fixed income—namely, a salary!

Earning & Employment

While many people dream of becoming rich overnight through an inheritance or the lottery, most of us will earn money the old-fashioned way—by working for it. Teens need to understand that employment is the main way of earning money and that certain behaviors enhance productivity while assuring that employment is more enjoyable and lucrative.

Earning pays big dividends.

By the time our kids become teens, they have received "easy money" many times in the form of gifts for birthdays, Christmas, or other special occasions. So why would they want to work for it? One key answer is financial independence. Helping teens embrace this concept will prepare them for the many years spent working for others or for themselves as business owners.

Work has many rewards.

Teens who loathe doing chores may not easily be convinced that earning money is a hot idea. Stressing the many rewards of work can help change teens' attitudes. So why do we work, really? Obviously, money is a key factor. We work because we need to earn money for things our families need and want. Teens desiring more than allowance money and gifts may eagerly seek the chance to work outside of the home.

key point
EMPLOY-MENT IS A GIFT AND BLESSING.

Many workers have found—and teens need to understand—that money is not enough to make employment enjoyable or fulfilling. Working provides nonmonetary rewards such as (1) the satisfaction of a job you enjoy, (2) the opportunity to help others through your gifts and talents, and (3) the knowledge that your employment, while maybe not ideal, is perfecting skills needed in a special field or providing money for present or future goals.

BIG BIBLE POINT

Proverbs 13:22 addresses financial inheritances but is applicable to any kind of "inheritance" a parent would like to leave a child. In terms of employment, discuss:

• Why can an employment inheritance (a good work ethic) often prove more valuable than money?

• What attitudes do employers value and reward? despise and punish?

• Does God really care about on-the-job performance?

"Happiness is not in the mere possession of money; it lies in the joy of achievement, in the thrill of creative effort."
—Franklin D. Roosevelt

Do you ascribe to the "do as I say, not as I do" adage? If so, know that studies show that teens actually follow the opposite path, mimicking the actions of their parents. That's why it's important to model a good work ethic, complete with attitudes and actions that inspire teens to work hard and well. Indeed, teens need to know we place a high value on employment. Even more, they need to know we consider employment a blessing—a gift from God that enables us to enjoy the many rewards of our physical labor.

Earning money shows responsibility.

key point

WORKING BREEDS RESPON- SIBILITY.

In a recent survey, 52 percent of students 13–18 said they worked during the past school year. If your teen works after school or during summers, he can reap several benefits. He will quickly learn that money doesn't grow on trees; it's a limited resource that can be increased through employment. He'll practice the art of juggling new or additional financial responsibilities while budgeting for transportation, lunch, entertainment, and other items. He will better understand (and hopefully respect) the time and energy you sacrificially expend while earning money to meet your family's varied needs.

key point

NURTURE A HEALTHY WORK ETHIC EARLY!

What's a good age for teens to begin working? The answer will vary depending on your teen's maturity and perhaps the financial needs of your household. Most preteens or young teens can start working part-time as soon as their parents permit. Some ideal beginner jobs include babysitting, pet sitting, lawn care, and snow removal. Discuss with your teen other attractive options and your expectations concerning viable employment and employers. Safety, as always, should be a key consideration.

PARENT POINTER

Remember the dread and joy of finding your first youth job? Share that story to help your teen overcome first-job fears and frustrations.

Jobs for preteens or younger teens can be found through word of mouth and by talking to friends and neighbors. Older teens can explore opportunities with fast-food restaurants and small businesses. Keep in mind that most states have specific requirements concerning the number of hours teens can work after school each week. Some states also require teens to complete applications for work permits. Without such "working papers," your teen will not be able to work in any formal employment setting.

BIG BIBLE POINT

Psalm 90:17 implies that God's favor can ensure that our work is effective and satisfying. Read this verse with your teen and discuss:

- Why is job satisfaction important to us? to God?

- How does God establish our work?

- How can prayer help your work attitudes?

Summer is a great time for teens to work. Consider these job-hunting tips:

❶ Consider summer youth employment programs.

❷ Start your job search early, since many jobs for teens are snapped up quickly.

❸ Ask others, including the vocational advisor at your teen's school and church members who may be able to help.

❹ Investigate local corporations, as many of them employ teens in various positions that often pay slightly more than minimum wage.

JOBS FOR TEENS

BABYSITTER

OFFICE HELP

LAWN CARE

LIFEGUARD

PET SITTER

NEWSPAPER DELIVERY

SHOVELING

WAITING TABLES

FAST-FOOD WORKER

We can earn through our enterprises.

It's quite possible for teens to take an idea for a product or service and turn it into a business opportunity. Business-minded teens can tap into an increasing number of resources, especially on the Internet. One of the best is Teen Business Link (www.sba.gov/teens), a website sponsored by the Small Business Administration (SBA). The SBA is the government agency dedicated to helping small businesses thrive. Teen Business Link provides ideas, tips, articles, and other resources to help youths succeed in business.

key point

TEENS CAN USE THEIR GIFTS & TALENTS.

75%

of high-school graduates go to college or formal training. Others may opt for starting their own service-oriented businesses or enterprises.

DID YOU KNOW ...

It is especially useful in helping teens understand the myriad costs (time, money, effort) associated with starting and running a business.

10.4% of teens responding to a 2005 survey expect to earn $1 million by age 40, a slight increase from the 8.1% of teens who voiced a similar expectation in 2004!

Every venture begins with an idea! Teens whose heads are filled with ideas for products and services will likely find it easy to picture themselves as entrepreneurs. Does that mean all other teens should shy away from earning money through self-owned opportunities? Absolutely not! If your teen dreams of starting a business but just can't pinpoint ideas, encourage her to seek wisdom from God, who can provide the needed inspiration. Proverbs 8:12 notes, *"I, wisdom, dwell together with prudence."*

WHAT GIFTS AND TALENTS COULD YOUR TEEN TURN INTO MONEY?

key point

SERVING IS GOD'S WORK FOR US, TOO!

Your teen needs to realize that some God-given ideas, like volunteering, don't include a paycheck. Nonmonetary benefits of volunteering include learning skills that lead to future part-time or career positions—as well as ways to sacrificially serve others. Tutoring benefits younger kids who desperately need to improve their grades in order to be promoted, while lawn care helps senior citizens who are physically unable to work in the yard themselves. Whatever your teen chooses to do, remind him that no good deed is ever wasted!

Working for oneself seems like a good idea, but it usually requires more time and energy than expected. Read Luke 14:28-30 with your teen and discuss the following:

✦ What are common or unique costs?

✦ Is soliciting help from others who have owned a business a good idea? Explain.

✦ Is it ever good to pass up an opportunity? Explain.

IN A RECENT SURVEY, PROFESSIONAL SPORTS WAS HIGH ON TEEN BOYS' CAREER ASPIRATIONS.

IDEAL CAREER	% TEEN BOYS	% TEEN GIRLS
Professional athlete	7.8	0.4
Computer-related job	7.4	2.1
Business	10.9	7.5

(Junior Achievement/Enterprise Poll)

We earn through accruing interest.

Many parents aren't comfortable talking about saving or investing money, since it spotlights their own (possibly less-than-perfect) savings habits. Despite this, it's important to teach your teen the benefits of saving money. An obvious benefit is having money available for planned purchases or emergency needs. Focusing on the future ensures we don't spend money on everything our hearts desire today. Earning interest is another plus of saving. Teens can appreciate that interest adds up to more money in the bank—without working for it! This "free money" accumulates over time, providing incentives not to withdraw funds on a whim.

MIDDLE-SCHOOL MEMOS

Many banks team with schools to offer savings accounts for which deposits can be made during school hours. Encourage your teen's participation by matching an initial deposit of up to $25.

Clearly, "out of sight, out of mind" is an underlying advantage of saving money! If it's not readily available, we can't spend it. While this promotes savings, teens may complain about the need to visit a bank or ATM to get funds. Counter by stressing that saving money encourages financial discipline—something we all need to master. Helping your teen develop savings goals may alleviate pressure to spend!

Remind your teen that money is hard to get—and easy to lose!

Every April, the American Banking Association Educational Foundation hosts "National Teach Children to Save Day." The annual event encourages local banks and credit unions to offer age-specific programs for kids and teens. Sponsoring organizations offer simple accounts, like passbook accounts, that help teens easily track deposits and withdrawals. They also provide information on how to fill out deposit and withdrawal slips, explain how to use ATM cards, and answer questions.

The following chart shows savings growth at a rate of 5 percent interest. Use it to help teens calculate their current savings or the amount and time needed to save for items.

Weekly Savings	After 1 year	After 2 years	After 3 years
$10	$532.64	$1,091.92	$1,679.16
$15	$798.97	$1,637.88	$2,518.74
$20	$1,065.29	$2,183.34	$3,358.32
$25	$1,331.61	$2,729.80	$4,197.90
$30	$1,597.93	$3,275.76	$5,037.48
$35	$1,864.26	$3,821.72	$5,877.06

Like adults, teens may need help saving money. The "pay yourself" method often works. Have teens save a specific percentage from every allowance or paycheck. Working teens whose employers offer direct deposit should take advantage of this benefit. In any case, a teen will be more likely to save if your family establishes a regular banking day for family banking needs.

While borrowing or lending money in an emergency may be necessary at some point, money can tear apart the best of friends. Talk to your teen about the pitfalls of borrowing from or lending to his friends.

Careers and jobs create choices.

Jobs and careers abound for today's teens! But choosing one may be difficult for teens who can't imagine spending the rest of their lives doing one type of work. Help your teen analyze his choices, showing him how to pinpoint tailor-made opportunities that allow for skill and income growth.

All work is honorable.

key point
THERE ARE NO WORTHLESS JOBS.

It has been said that there are no menial jobs, just menial people. The inference is that all work is honorable, despite attitudes to the contrary. When we help our kids develop proper attitudes about work, we allow them to explore diverse opportunities. Teens notice whether we criticize or applaud other peoples' jobs. Especially noticeable are contemptuous attitudes toward lower-wage earners.

"The sum of wisdom is that time is never lost that is devoted to work."
— Ralph Waldo Emerson

POINTER

How you really feel about certain types of jobs will show as your teen looks at possible opportunities. Ask God to help you be more open to positions that you'd never want to do but that your teen might enjoy or be good at.

One clue to work attitudes is looking at how we treat people in service positions, including wait staff and housekeeping or custodial personnel. Discuss with your teen if people treat her respectfully and appreciatively or with rudeness and disregard. Remind your teen that we're to respect people—not worship certain jobs or money!

Answers to these questions help reveal how we really treat people—and unveil the negative legacy we may be inadvertently passing on to our teens. As Christians, we should know that all work can honor God, who blesses us with varying positions based on our abilities, talents, and other criteria. Teens need to learn that many factors affect job positions and pay—many out of workers' control.

> "We make a living by what we get, but we make a life by what we give."
> —Winston Churchill

Discuss the meaning of this quote with your teen. Chat about how work and serving are both honorable when done for others—and for God!

BIG BIBLE POINT

Laziness undermines efforts to earn money. Read Proverbs 6:6-11 with your teen, then discuss:

• How do these verses relate to employment?

• What excuses do people give for not working?

• What attitudes or behaviors can cause people to become sluggards over time?

• What qualities ensure job success?

WHAT ATTITUDES ABOUT WORK AND WORK ETHIC ARE YOU GIVING YOUR TEEN?

Proverbs 14:23 declares that *"all hard work brings a profit, but mere talk leads only to poverty."* Teach your teen the difference between the two and how hard work brings rewards. Help her appreciate any job that enables her to earn wages, while encouraging her to choose a specific employment path that matches her interests, gifts, and talents. In so doing, you'll help guide her to work she can enjoy for years to come!

key point
HARD WORK BRINGS VALUABLE REWARDS!

Match your interests with your employment.

Earning money is one thing; earning it in a job or career that interests you is another. We usually think of "dead-end" jobs or careers as those that hold little interest, offer little or no room for advancement, and offer low pay. Conversely, dream positions usually top the interest, advancement, and salary scales. But remember that one person's dream may be another's nightmare! It's important for teens to match *their* interests (not ours) with chosen employment.

key point
ENCOURAGE TEENS TO TRY NEW JOB IDEAS!

Here are a few tips to achieving job satisfaction. Share and discuss them with your teen!

1.
Do what you love. If your teen dislikes animals, it would be unwise to seek work with an animal shelter or vet clinic. List your interests, then try matching jobs to the list.

2.
Relax—and think of your job as recreation! Teens who enjoy sports might enjoy working as an aide at a summer camp or coaching junior baseball.

3.
Try something new! Variety adds spice to life—and increases the chance that teens will find jobs or career paths they may never have considered before.

"Nothing will work unless you do." — Maya Angelou

FASTEST-GROWING CAREERS
FOR COLLEGE GRADS

Computer software engineer

Physician's assistant

Network communication

Medical records & information

Physical therapist

What should you do if your teen knows her interests but can't find a job to match? Remind her that the marketplace is always changing. A case in point is the Internet. Few people expected the Internet to become such a big deal, spurring new jobs and business opportunities. Although a specific job may not yet define what your teen hopes to do someday, encourage her to acquire skills that easily translate to different environments and industries.

Your teen needs to see that you're satisfied with your work or actively trying to change positions in order to achieve job satisfaction. Monitor the way you talk about your positions, pay, supervisors, and other work-related issues. But paint a balanced picture. Some things we do will go unappreciated or rewarded, and some bosses are difficult to work with. That's life. Teens should be prepared for both situations but stay focused on doing the best job possible—always.

College helps prepare teens and twenty-somethings for a lifetime of job satisfaction!

CAREER CHOICES

What's hot, what's not & what's new in today's (and tomorrow's) job market!

Trying to decide what's the best career course or job for you? Then you need to know what's going on in the job market! Five of the ten fastest-growing occupations in North America are health-related. Computers and business services are also great choices for today—and tomorrow!

TOP 10 FUTURE JOBS

1. PERSONAL AND HOME-CARE AIDES

2. GENERAL HEALTH AIDES

3. SYSTEMS ANALYSTS

4. COMPUTER ENGINEERS

5. PHYSICAL-THERAPY ASSISTANTS

6. COMPUTER OPERATORS

7. OCCUPATIONAL THERAPISTS

8. PHYSICAL THERAPISTS

9. RESIDENTIAL COUNSELORS

10. HUMAN-SERVICES WORKERS

U.S. Department of Labor's Occupational Outlook Handbook

INTERESTS	CAREER & JOB IDEAS
ANIMALS	pet sitter, dog walker, zookeeper, veterinarian, groomer, trainer
COSMETOLOGY	hair stylist, barber, beautician, makeup artist
COMPUTERS	programmers, analysts, engineers, technicians, software designers
FOOD	chef, caterer, baker, dietician, food critic, school cafeteria manager
MAINTENANCE	automobile service, appliance repair, machinery technician
MEDICINE & HEALTH	doctor, registered nurse, pharmacist, psychiatrist, paramedic, home health care
MONEY & FINANCE	banker, accountant, auditor, payroll manager, stock broker, tax advisor
PEOPLE	human-resources manager, minister, tour guide, child or senior care, teacher
TRAVEL	pilot, cruise-ship worker, travel writer, missionary, concierge
SPORTS	athlete, coach, physical therapist, fitness trainer, golf-course superintendent
WRITING	author, technical writer, journalist, poet, reporter, language teacher

"NEVER WORK JUST FOR
MONEY OR FOR POWER. THEY
WON'T SAVE YOUR SOUL OR
HELP YOU SLEEP AT NIGHT."
— *MARIAN WRIGHT EDELMAN*

Education is tied to employment.

School-adverse teens often view employment as a means of escaping the rigors of academic work. Despite this, challenge teens to pursue the level of education or training required for preferred jobs or careers. Provide incentive by helping your teen understand the link between education and salary. Generally, jobs pay higher salaries for higher levels of education or training. Teens can expect to earn more money when they hold vocational certifications or college degrees.

key point
EDUCATION IS LINKED TO SALARY.

PARENT POINTER

The fast track usually isn't. Share with your teen son or daughter how much time and effort it has taken you to reach your present salary level or position. Remind your teen that good things require patience—including a good job or career!

An increasing number of employers expect applicants to have at least a college degree. For some fields, like computer technology, job seekers need to earn advanced certifications in specific skills. Better educated or trained workers usually pick and choose the type of work they do, while enjoying higher pay and increased advancement opportunities. Workers who are unhappy in their jobs can obtain additional education to catapult into new positions or careers.

Teens need to realize that school is the key to better jobs and more secure futures!

Online classes make sense and offer flexibility.

Today, many college-bound teens can take classes via the Internet as colleges expand online offerings. It's possible to work in some fields by obtaining a more affordable level of schooling and then returning later to finish a degree. Starting out as a paralegal or legal secretary, for example, provides valuable law experience prior to attending law school.

TRY THIS!

Read 1 John 5:14, 15 with your teen. Discuss how seeking God can be related to schooling and job choices.

Higher education is costly, but internships, scholarships, and other programs can make education more affordable. Some employers offer financial aid, while some churches offer members-only scholarships. College work-study programs are another viable option. Clearly, where there's a will there may be a way. Help your teen keep this in mind while exploring opportunities.

Teens with a stay-at-home parent or a parent with a home business may dream of doing the same. Yet they may not understand the financial sacrifices or planning it can take. If you or your spouse transitioned from the workplace to home in either capacity, talk to your teen about how your family was able to achieve this goal.

Being employed requires etiquette.

Being employed means more than just showing up for work and getting paid. Instead of a crash course, teens need ongoing help with etiquette to avoid pitfalls that undermine employability. While teens may shun your opinion in other areas, this may be one in which they welcome your advice!

First impressions at interviews *do* count!

Y*ou won't get a second chance to make a first impression.* At no time does that adage ring truer than during job interviews! After successfully applying for a job, teens must be ready for this job-search phase. Circumventing interviews is impossible, even for positions with a company a parent may work for. Teaching teens to properly prepare for, and participate in, interviews equips them with the tools necessary to land part-time jobs and career positions.

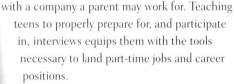

Tattoos, body piercings, and multicolored hair can thwart interview efforts. Explain to your teen that employers may not agree with these kinds of individual expressions in the workplace even though they may be fine at home or with friends.

Even before an interview, a teen will need an effective résumé. Résumés should include relevant job experience, related skills, and educational background. Include any community service activities, such as scouting or tutoring, that show initiative or leadership. Teens should take résumé preparation as seriously as studying for SATs—remembering to get help if needed and never to lie on résumés!

key point
INTERVIEWS REQUIRE YOUR BEST!

Effective interviewing skills can stick with teens through life, enabling them to successfully land career positions. Interviewing encompasses verbal and nonverbal skills such as enunciation, posture, and eye contact. Dress is another important factor. A conservative outfit usually works best. Guys should opt for dark pants rather than jeans and switch athletic shoes for basic dress shoes (rubber heels are acceptable). Teen girls should don simple tops rather than revealing ones and slacks or skirts that flatter without being tight.

TRY THIS!

Hold a mock inteview at home before your teen has his or her first interview with a potential employer. Rehearse what to wear, how to shake hands, what to say, and closing the interview with a smile!

INTERVIEW **BUSTERS!**

BOTTOMS	TOPS	ACCESSORIES	OTHER
• blue jeans	• sweatshirts	• facial piercings	• wild hairdos
• shorts	• T-shirts	• nose rings	• body odor
• skimpy skirts	• halter tops	• tongue studs	• dirty nails
• holes in pants	• tank tops	• excessive rings	• bad breath
• ragged hems	• revealing	or other jewelry	• chomping gum
• tight pants	anything!	• tattoos	
		• casual sandals	
		or filp-flops	

Talking to teens about their appearance can prove explosive at times. But it must be done *before* they begin interviewing. If your teen questions your advice, seek help from a trusted family member or friend. And if needed, give your teen money to augment an unsuitable wardrobe.

Experts warn that even on casual days, you shouldn't dress down totally.

45

Interviews require preparation!

key point

INTERVIEWS ARE LIKE INVITATIONS.

An interview can be a scary thing for a teen who isn't sure what to expect. Remind your teen that an interview is an invitation—and an indication that a company wants to see an applicant. Both parties can relax knowing this is not a hostile meeting but a chance to get to know each other while determining whether a decision to hire could prove a win-win situation. Experience and skills are important, but enthusiasm and initiative are also essential. Encourage your teen to be as personable and polite as possible.

TRY THIS!

Seeing is believing! Try videotaping a mock interview, then watch it with your teen. Point out any bloopers and offer suggestions for improvement.

Squelch fears by walking your teen through the interview process, emphasizing common elements found in all job interviews. Analyze the meeting from the greeting to the closing. What happens during each stage? What actions or attitudes make or break interviews? It's important for teens to know that, although they have submitted a résumé, they'll have to complete an application. Surf the Internet for a sample job application to help your son or daughter visualize what's required.

Does your teen have a physical, mental, or emotional challenge that may limit employability? If so, job preparation and training are available through various state and federal programs. Surf online or check your phone directory for assistance.

Explain that interview questions are designed to learn more about an applicant's experience, skills, and work-related habits and attitudes.

key point
PRACTICE MAKES PERFECT!

Encourage your teen to answer honestly—even when asked about her weaknesses. Point out that a quick note expressing thanks for an interview is always in good taste.

7 STEPS TO BUILDING A BETTER RÉSUMÉ!

OBJECTIVE	Begin with a sentence or two identifying job prospects and, when possible, tie them to special skills.
CAPABILITIES	Specify the skills that relate to the preferred job or industry. Bulleted lists work well.
EXPERIENCE	Include all dates and positions, ensuring any long gaps are explained during the interview. Include responsibilities.
COMMUNITY SERVICE	Teens with limited work experience can highlight school, church, or civic involvement or list special recognitions or awards.
SKILLS	Highlight job skills such as word-processing, computers (software and hardware), and working with relevant equipment.
EDUCATION	Mention schools you've attended; highlight any special recognition, achievements, or awards.
REFERENCES	You may use "Available upon request," but have a list of names and contact information for professionals (including pastors) and teachers who can provide character references.

TRY THIS!

One of the best ways to perfect interviewing skills is to have a dress rehearsal and cover expected questions and answers. Practice shaking hands, smiling, pausing, and holding eye contact as often as needed to feel confident and prepared.

Etiquette on the job is important.

Galatians 5:16 tells us to live by the Spirit and not gratify the desires of our sinful natures. What a powerful reminder of how we rely on God's help to overcome ungodly attitudes and behaviors, including those necessary for an effective work life. We can be leaders in workplace etiquette, exhibiting attitudes and actions worth emulating.

BIG BIBLE POINT

Read aloud Ephesians 4:29 and James 3:10 with your teen. Discuss how both verses can be used at any job. Visit about the importance of kind, courteous behavior at work and in public.

key point
JOBS REQUIRE OUR BEST BEHAVIOR!

key point
IMPRESS "THE BOSS" WITH GOOD ETIQUETTE.

PARENT POINTER

Think for a moment about the way you act at work. Your behavior hardly resembles what it did when you were young. Keep this in mind as you patiently help your teen shape attitudes and behaviors befitting the workplace.

Teens need to know that expectations exist concerning their workplace behavior. Not only does God expect them to follow certain guidelines, but so will employers. Like schools, employers have specific, stated guidelines they expect all employees to adhere to. Failure to do so can result in corrective action and even dismissal. Being a teen is no excuse. When we teach teens to act maturely with supervisors, co-workers, and others, we help them enjoy easier work relationships.

Two key areas to highlight are *attendance* and *courtesy*. Both of these are nonnegotiable. It should come as no surprise to teens that they are expected to show up at agreed-upon days and times and may even have to "clock in" or complete timesheets. Challenge your teen to record time accurately and honestly—always! Let him know that excessive absences and tardiness are frowned upon and often lead to reprimands or dismissal. Teens must expect to treat co-workers, customers, clients, and others with respect—even during disagreements.

TARGET MOMENT

Remind your teen that most employers have "no tolerance" rules concerning drug use and may conduct periodic drug testing.

MIDDLE-SCHOOL MEMOS

Chores help prepare kids for managing time at work. Prepare a chart with about two hours of household chores. Have your teen follow the chart using a timer. Discuss the results and why good planning and managing time are important work skills.

Remind your teen that lunch and other breaks should not exceed allotted times.

29% of all workers eat at their desks

25% of all workers eat in work lunchrooms

30% of all workers eat at home

Professionalism is often a gray area. When in doubt, teens should consult supervisors to assure they're adhering to policies regarding attire and conduct. A work environment is not a playground or amusement park, so teens should avoid immature behavior and wasting time. This includes chatting on cell phones, being loud with co-workers, and being away from work areas.

Paychecks provide opportunities.

Money is a necessity, and earning it on a regular basis helps us meet ongoing needs. A recurring paycheck helps us plan how to allocate for daily and monthly expenses. It can have the same beneficial affect on teens who learn that a paycheck only stretches so far—and no further!

Paychecks allow us to keep earning.

Cha-ching! Knowing that a regular paycheck is coming in can be music to teens' ears! They need money to pay for various items on their wants and needs lists, and receiving a paycheck fits the bill. Before working, kids look to their parents as primary sources of money. Once regular paychecks began to roll in, we can begin weaning them from financial dependency. Insist that teens take a more active role by paying most or all associated costs for items on "must-have" lists.

key point
PAYCHECKS HELP US ACCOMPLISH GOALS.

By exercising their purchasing power, teens can appreciate how freeing, yet limiting, a paycheck is. As your teen experiences the thrill of bringing home a paycheck, challenge him to think before he spends, considering needs before wants and ensuring he sets aside funds to tithe and save. Help your teen develop a simple budget of expenses such as lunch, clothes, and transportation so he knows how much money *not* to spend out of each paycheck.

BUDGETS HELP
S-T-R-E-T-C-H
DOLLARS—PASS ON GOOD BUDGETING HABITS!

Your favorite accronym might be TGIP, for "Thank Goodness It's Payday"! The thrill associated with the day we receive earned wages can be dimmed by thoughts of how we've already planned to spend our money. Help your teen realize that such an emotional roller coaster on payday may exist, but careful planning can help—and remembering that it's "In God We Trust!"

Take the mystery out of "taxing matters." Surf with your teen to the IRS's web site at *www.irs. gov/individuals* for current information for students.

key point
PAYCHECKS CREATE CHOICES FOR US.

BIG BIBLE POINT

Read Matthew 17:24-27 aloud with your teen then discuss these tax-related questions.

❖ What benefits do we receive from our taxes?

❖ What did Jesus do when confronted with taxes?

❖ What does Jesus' example teach us?

AVOID IDENTITY THEFT!

Limit the personal information you carry with you.

Don't give financial info or social security numbers over phones.

Lock up purses or wallets while working.

Shred mail, bills, and receipts before tossing.

Keep an up-to-date list, safely stored at home, of credit cards and contact information.

As teens earn wages and have more financial information to protect, they need to know about identity theft, the fastest growing white-color crime. An identity thief steals personal data and uses it to obtain cash from bank or credit-card accounts. Even if the thief is caught, a teen may be responsible for the debt and have difficulty reestablishing a good credit history. Encourage your teen to protect his personal information on pay stubs, his driver's license, and credit cards. For more on identity theft, surf to the Federal Trade Commission's website at www.consumer.gov/idtheft.

Plan for paychecks before receiving them.

Where did my money go? Ever feel like this after getting paid and seeing the various deductions taken from your paycheck? What a reality check! Teens need to be prepared for the same. Help your working teen understand the difference between gross and net pay and why weekly income is not what he will actually bring home. Prepare him for the shock of seeing his income reduced by withholdings for taxes, possible health or dental benefits, and other items. And remind your teen that, unless his employer offers direct deposit, he is responsible for cashing or depositing his paychecks.

key point
PLAN FOR PAYCHECKS—AND FOR SPENDING!

Paychecks seem to disappear quickly if they're not properly planned for!

Teens often have trouble understanding how paychecks and biblical principles are related. Proverbs 13:11 says, *"Dishonest money dwindles away, but he who gathers money little by little makes it grow."* Discuss these questions.

❖ How does this verse relate to paychecks and working honestly?

❖ How can savings be the answer for questions about future purchases?

❖ How does not being honest with your employer about times worked or the quality of your effort cheat you both?

❖ What does this verse teach about the value of patience and hard work?

"Money earned with pains should be spent on pleasure"
(Chinese proverb). Have a fun fund!

key point
PAYCHECKS ARE PERSONAL.

Explain to teens that it's not a good idea to share salary information with co-workers. Salary differences often spark envy and strife. Help your teen avoid pay-related issues by keeping her salary, raises, and other financial information confidential. Also, help your teen realize that mistakes can happen even on paychecks. For your teen's first few paychecks, help determine whether the amount is accurate by checking if the correct hourly rate was given. If mistakes occur, encourage your son or daughter to talk to the boss or payroll representative about how to correct the error.

Teens often are so excited by the prospect of incoming money that they blow it on things they don't need—and run short on things they *do* need! Remind your teen that a budget can help in spending earned money responsibly. Prior planning for where money is to be spent and saved is key when teens begin earning their own paychecks. Help your teen avoid the pattern of living paycheck to paycheck because of poor planning! Remind your teen to avoid buying with credit to make it to the next paycheck. Budgeting spending is much wiser!

Remind your teen that money doesn't grow on trees—it's hard to earn and easy to lose!

✓ Are your own spending habits under control? Do you use credit too often instead of exercising patience? Your teen watches not only what you buy but how you pay for it. Choose and use credit carefully. The more you model "patience in purchasing," the more your teen will, too!

Spending & Serving Today

What does spending money mean to you? Buying whatever is on your wish list? Investing for retirement? Tithing and charitable giving? None of the above? All of the above? How you and your family define "spending" will shape the way your teen saves and spends her own money.

There's more to spending than just buying.

Like everything else we have, our money is a gift from God. We can show our appreciation for it by being good stewards of our money. Teaching your teen to do the same empowers him to develop beneficial spending and giving patterns that influence patterns throughout his adulthood.

We can spend, save, *and* serve.

In just five years, from 1999 to 2004, teen spending jumped almost 40 percent, from $122 billion to $169 billion! The number represents two types of purchases: those teens made and those teens influenced adults to make. Figures like this make it imperative that we talk with teens not only about spending money but also about choices and spending wisely. Help your teen understand that there's an "opportunity cost" associated with every decision. In other words, a dollar spent on a purchase is no longer available to save, invest, or donate.

There are three main ways to use money.

1. SPEND
2. SAVE
3. SERVE

Help your teen embrace a broad definition of managing money so he doesn't focus just on buying.

key point
SPENDING & SAVING REQUIRE CHOICES.

One study found that young adults are saving about 25 percent more than in the past—but most young people tend to save money just long enough to purchase big-ticket items.

That approach to saving is not necessarily bad, but it may not be the most effective savings plan for older teens saving for college or first cars. An option to encourage steady, secure savings for teen are certificates of deposit (CDs). These investments offer good interest rates while discouraging withdrawals via penalties.

Disposable income is the amount of money we have left after taxes. Remind your teen that disposable doesn't mean using our money until it's all gone!

Serving others is one way to thank God for blessing us financially. Encourage your teen to think of ways he could use his money to serve, such as purchasing canned goods for soup kitchens or donating to outreach programs or missionaries. Challenge him to set aside a portion of each paycheck or allowance to help someone needy. Remind your teen that sharing his good fortune serves others—and God!

Read Luke 12:13-21. Then discuss the rich man's focus for his money and how his actions proved he was greedy, not generous.

DISCUSS THESE WITH YOUR TEEN. HOW DO YOU BOTH MEASURE UP?

1. You live for payday or allowance day!
2. You often dream about what you want to buy.
3. You can't seem to make money last for long.
4. You rarely have money left to save or donate.
5. You don't keep track of your spending or have a budget.
6. Having a lot of money makes you feel good inside.
7. You rarely buy things for others.

Identify and prioritize needs and wants.

By the time our kids are toddlers, they've become adept at expressing their needs and wants. At the same time, we've become adept at identifying differences between the two to make sure our kids receive those things they absolutely need to grow and develop into healthy individuals: things like nutritious food, clothing, and love—and fun stuff like toys, books, games, and even snacks. Some might not be classified as deep-felt needs, but they do help make life better!

key point
NEEDS ARE ESTABLISHED EARLY IN LIFE.

Prioritizing needs and wants is a must if we're to avoid most money problems, including excessive debt, bankruptcy, and poverty. Teens need to understand the importance of prioritizing needs and wants. Teaching your teen this balancing act won't be easy—and she may not like going without things she really wants. But delayed gratification has its rewards, including learning how to use money wisely for basic needs without going into debt or borrowing.

key point
WE CAN'T HAVE ALL THAT WE DESIRE!

Read aloud with your teen Matthew 7:7-11 and Luke 11:3. Then discuss:

• What do these verses promise regarding God's provision for our needs?
• Do they also relate to our wants? If so, how?
• What "good gifts" does your family need? How can you help God provide for them?

God's Word tells us that God cares about providing for our needs. Jesus taught his disciples to pray for daily bread, and Paul assured us that God meets our needs in Christ. If Scripture places such emphasis on needs over wants, shouldn't we do the same?

PARENT POINTER

Help your teen recognize that your family's needs must be met first and essential necessities not forgotten. Model good prioritizing skills, and your teen will follow your example!

TARGET MOMENT

How much money a person has will dictate how he uses money to obtain necessities like food and housing. With your teen, list ways to meet basic needs more affordably.

Insurance is an investment that often gets pushed to the bottom of our priorities. But medical and dental insurance can actually prove cost-effective—even for teens. And car insurance, as teens begin to be mobile, is a must. But cars and car insurance aside, what other things do teens spend their money on each day? Check out this chart for some real surprises!

WHAT ARE TEENS BUYING?

	Females	Males
1. CLOTHES	43%	21%
2. FOOD	31%	30%
3. SNACKS & POP	34%	24%
4. CDs & MUSIC	18%	19%
5. LUNCH (school days)	22%	13%
6. SHOES	16%	15%
7. VIDEO GAMES	5%	18%
8. JEWELRY	15%	7%
9. MAGAZINES	12%	9%
10. ICE CREAM	10%	7%

CHECK IT OUT!

As today's teens age, their yearly discretionary income increases from nearly $1,500 at age 13 to about $4,500 by age 17. That's a lot of spending power!

Budgets help us spend carefully.

If we're honest, most of us don't spend money as carefully as we could. Sometimes we feel the desire to splurge on an unplanned shopping trip or family outing. Or a friend or co-worker encourages an impromptu meal or other activity. If this happens continually, we can find ourselves strapped for cash, even though we may make enough money to meet our family's needs. The solution? We need to establish a plan of action, or budget, that details how we spend our money—and it's important to teach our teens to do the same.

key point
BUDGETS HELP CONTROL SPENDING.

MONEY TO GIVE OR TITHE

AMOUNT YOU EARN MONTHLY

FACTORS IN BUDGETING YOUR MONEY

PLANNED SAVINGS EACH MONTH

MONTHLY EXPENSES

Budgets help us track income and expenses. Granted, budgeting is akin to dieting in some people's minds and equally unappetizing. But the reality is that a budget enables you to track spending, saving, and serving down to the last penny.

Have your teen make a grocery list, then shop within a specified budget. Discuss how well you stuck to the budget, how it affected your needs and wants, and how it saved you money.

Like any financial tool, a budget should be specific, measurable, and achievable. In other words, discourage your teen from making his budget so strict that sticking to it is impossible! Explain to your teen that a good budget lists all money coming in during the month and all expenses. Remind your teen that a budget needs to include the following categories:

❶ **DAILY AND MONTHLY EXPENSES** (car payment, insurance, lunches, gasoline)

❷ **SAVINGS** (for goals and emergencies—even a small, consistent amount is needed)

❸ **ENTERTAINMENT** (for movies, video rentals, CDs, snacks)

❹ **GIVING OR SERVING** (tithing, church offerings, donations)

Teens can learn that budgets help control spending, assure saving, and ease the pain of being broke!

Explain to your teen that a bottom-line figure for monthly spending emerges when all expenses are subtracted from income. If the expenses far outweigh one's income, adjustments are needed in spending. Point out that unexpected expenses can upset the best budgeting efforts. The solution is to implement an emergency fund for which money is set aside for such situations.

Spending requires dollars and "sense."

Spending responsibly helps reduce the likelihood of using money—or credit—recklessly. Of course, it's okay to budget for things we dream of having, but dreams will become financial nightmares if we don't budget and spend wisely.

Plan your purchases carefully.

How do you feel about Russian roulette, the deadly game of chance? Most of us wouldn't go there! The risk is too high and the consequences too severe. Yet when you think of it, spending money without planning is akin to playing Russian roulette—and the consequences are just as dire!

key point
SPENDING CREATES CONSEQUENCES.

REMIND YOUR TEEN THAT ...

Money is like time—it can be wasted or invested, but once spent, it is impossible (usually) to get back!

Has this ever happened to you? You run to the store to buy a few items, but before long you've switched from a hand basket to a cart, never saw the express lane, and spent way more than you planned? Next, you and your spouse argue about the amount spent. Finally, you search your brain for ways to come up with the needed cash to pay a bill because you've overspent at the supermarket. The worse case scenario: you pay that bill using a credit card.

7 OUT OF **10** TEENS HAVE ACCESS TO CREDIT CARDS!

How can a simple shopping trip turn into such a financial meltdown? Impulse spending! If we're ever going to teach our teens to have control over their finances, it's important that we help them consistently stick to a budget.

40% of American families live on 110% of their incomes.

Plan a budgeting session with your teen to discuss your family's budget. Share ways you can stick to financial goals.

TRY THIS!

Teens love eating out. Give your teen a gift certificate or gift card to a favorite fast-food restaurant, encouraging her to use it for budgeting fast-food purchases.

Sure, we can throw in an occasional treat, but when the treat becomes the norm it's likely that we will never control spending, meet financial goals, or stay debt free. On the upside, we can do better with God's help. The apostle James likened the tongue to "a world of iniquity" that no man can tame but inferred that God can. Similarly, God can help us tame our spending. Invite him to do so!

The sooner our teens learn to tame spending, the easier it will be for them to maintain control over money matters. Encourage your teen to spend within limits imposed by herself or by you. Show tough love. Put the brakes on bailing your teen out whenever she runs out of cash from allowances or paychecks. Encourage her to make wise choices using common sense to keep the most of her *cents* whenever possible!

TEENS ARE A GROWING MARKET!
The teen population will expand over a million in the next few years. Imagine the spending power—and choices— our teens will face in the future!

32.4 million in 2000

33.5 million in 2010

Debt destroys financial freedom!

Like money, debt is a tool that enables us to obtain some of the things we want or need. Whether debt is viewed as good or bad depends on how it is used and its influence on our lifestyle. A mortgage is considered good debt because it enables us to buy a home. Bad debt can be harder to define because it may not be inherently bad, although it is often unnecessary. Payday loans fit this category, and most experts agree that payday loans should be avoided!

> **key point**
> **AVOID PAYDAY LOANS— PLAN WELL!**

> **key point**
> **SOME DEBT IS UNAVOIDABLE.**

Debt is a tool that enables us to buy homes, cars, and other dream purchases. But use debt—and debit and credit cards—wisely!

Explain to your teen that most of us dream of paying cash for a car or home, but the reality is that won't happen. We simply don't have thousands— or hundreds of thousands—of dollars lying around! The solution is to take out a loan for these items. As long as we stay within reasonable boundaries, such debt usually is more a bless- ing than a curse. Problems arise when we take out loans that require payments beyond our ability to pay!

> **key point**
> **DON'T BECOME A SLAVE TO DEBT!**

> *Debt may not seem a big deal to teens only calculating the amount of a loan or credit-card balance. Help them see the bigger picture by talking to them about interest. Teens need to understand that interest is either earned (on savings) or paid (on debts). Calculating interest into a payment can help teens see more clearly how costly being in debt really is!*

Teens need to understand that debt creates opportunities for us to get what we want or need, but it's not free money, since we must pay back borrowed funds—plus more. Interest on loans and credit cards increase the amount of money we owe. Plus, the more debt we have, the greater the amount of income needed to pay debts off. Training teens to handle debt responsibly means modeling appropriate behavior. When teens see us relying on God rather than debt to meet family needs, they also learn to trust God to meet their needs and to provide for at least some of their wants.

Teens model your spending habits. Set healthy examples when using loans, extended credit, and charge cards!

Help your teen see how interest adds to debt. Show your teen your loan or credit-card statements and discuss ways to pay off debt quickly, without incurring additional debt for a season.

Proverbs 22:6 is an encouragement for parents who "train a child in the way he should go." However, the following verse warns that "the rich rule over the poor, and the borrower is servant to the lender." Owing money makes us servants to banks and other institutions as we work to pay off debt. If we don't, we may lose the very purchases we sought to gain! Foreclosures or seizures not only ruin credit history but also make us vulnerable to feelings of inadequacy or low self-esteem. Make a concerted effort to help your teen learn to avoid the negative consequences of poor debt handling!

Stay debt free for as long as possible!

When we handle debt carefully, we pass along a valuable lesson to our children, that debt is not kids' play! While some debt is unavoidable, teens should be challenged to stay debt free as long as possible. Teach teens about the dangers of debt, while encouraging them to use debt wisely but sparingly. Help them see that most debts should be avoided until teens can really afford related payments, and even then teens should think twice before obtaining certain kinds of debt, especially credit cards.

key point
ALWAYS USE DEBT SPARINGLY.

TARGET MOMENT

The next time a credit-card solicitation arrives, seize the opportunity to talk about the ease of getting credit cards, yet the difficulty in getting debt free if they're abused.

When you regularly use credit cards for presents, your teen will learn to do the same. Establish a budget for such items. Better yet, use special bank accounts to save for birthdays, holidays, and other gift-giving.

Talking to teens about credit cards and debit cards is better done sooner than later. Talk with yours about the benefits and dangers of credit-card use. Benefits include convenience of shopping for pricey items and paying for emergency purchases, like car tires. A key danger entails running up balances that cannot be easily or quickly paid off. Another danger is maxing out one card, then getting another just to have access to ready "cash."

Help your teen get a grip on credit cards. Explain that a credit card is not free money, but a loan that must be repaid with interest. Interest accrues on outstanding balances, meaning your teen will be responsible for the original payment plus extra. That extra is what makes credit cards so expensive, since most interest is well over 17 percent!

Read Ecclesiastes 5:10 with your teen and discuss how the verse relates to accumulating debt and constantly spending money.

If your teen is tempted to use credit, remind him of these important reali-

A recent study found that one in three high-school students uses credit cards regularly.

ties: (1) if he doesn't have money today, he probably won't have it when the bill arrives; (2) paying balances avoids interest costs; (3) lay-away plans are a better choice; (4) deferred payments can mess up future budgets; and (5) cash advances often have heftier interest fees than actual credit-card purchases.

AVERAGE CREDIT-CARD DEBT FOR AMERICAN HOUSEHOLDS WITH AT LEAST ONE CREDIT CARD

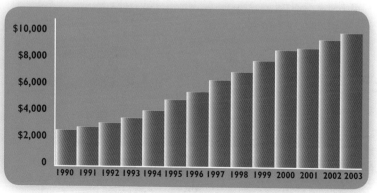

Paying for college takes planning.

Just the thought of paying college costs can be intimidating both for parens and their teens! Careful planning can make the difference between your teen attending college and missing a lifetime of educational benefits. Ideally, planning should begin long before a teen reaches high school, but a later start does not put college out of reach. Your teen may have to reduce spending, forgo planned purchases, or find other financing solutions in order to make college a reality.

College tuition takes careful planning for your teen—and your family.

Each college has scholarships not offered by other schools. Check catalogs and ask college financial-aid staff for school-specific scholarships for which your college-bound teen may be eligible.

Help your teen establish a plan for paying college costs and budget accordingly. College-bound teens need to be adept at budgeting *before* they leave home so that money they earn, financial-aid funds, or money from parents is well managed. Encourage your teen to research available grants. Filling out application forms is tedious, but each dollar received is worth the cost!

5 WISE WAYS TO SAVE AT COLLEGE!

BUY USED TEXTBOOKS.

LIVE AT HOME, IF POSSIBLE.

COOK INSTEAD OF EATING OUT.

REAPPLY FOR GRANTS.

USE A BIKE OR BUS — PARK THE CAR!

$20,000
IS THE AVERAGE DEBT LOAD FOR A 4-YEAR COLLEGE GRADUATE!

Beyond scholarships, other financial aid may be available for your teen. A very necessary first step will be completing a *Free Application for Federal Student Aid* (FAFSA) to determine eligibility for state and federal programs. Most financial aid is based on your income, and factors such as owning a home may also reduce the amount of aid offered to your teen. A federal guaranteed student loan is another option that offers lower interest rates than a bank loan. Explain to your teen that, unlike grants, loans of any kind must be paid back with interest.

To learn more about FAFSA, see www.fafsa. ed.gov.

CHECK THIS OUT!

Prepaid college savings accounts help pay for tuition at current rates and offer tax-free savings. Talk to a financial planner or banker about investing today for college tomorrow!

Combined tuition and meals are the largest college-related expense teens need to be aware of, but they're not the only ones. Books and school supplies, transportation, and general living expenses must be added to the overall costs for college-bound students. Help teens brainstorm how to pay for these. For example, buying used books at college bookstores or online can help curb the costs of textbooks. Financial gifts for birthdays or special occasions also can be saved for college use. Finally, part-time wages can go a long way to meeting costs for a college-bound teen.

BIG BIBLE POINT

Read Proverbs 13:7 with your teen and discuss the following.

- Why do some people pretend to be better off financially than they are?
- Which man probably handles his finances more wisely? Explain.

Even our money belongs to God.

Do we believe that God provides everything we have, or do we get it by our own strength or smarts? And if God does provide for our finances, who owns them? It's important to teach our teens that even our money belongs to God!

Serve only one master — serve God!

Psalm 62:10 advises, "Do not trust in extortion or take pride in stolen goods; though your riches increase, do not set your heart on them." Extortion and theft are clearly sinful. But what about setting our hearts on riches? Do we regularly challenge our teens not to set their eyes on earning money just for the sake of having it? Do we discuss ways they can put money to good use by serving others? Being good stewards of the money God allows us is key to our financial— and spiritual—health.

key point
BEING A GOOD STEWARD IS OFTEN DIFFICULT.

Our actions and attitudes speak volumes as our teens look to us for help in prioritizing needs and wants. One area worth examining is our attitude toward making additional income. Sometimes opportunities exist to make extra money. How we prioritize the way we spend extra cash reveals what's in our hearts. For example, earning extra funds to participate in a missions trip or afford a family vacation tells teens that helping others and family fun are both important.

> "No one can serve two masters. Either he will hate the one and love the other, or he will be devoted to the one and despise the other. You cannot serve both God and Money" (Matthew 6:24).

Discuss this verse with your teen by asking:

✤ Why can we not serve both God and money?

✤ Why do you think the word Money is capitalized?

✤ How can we serve God with our money?

"Store up for yourselves treasures in heaven.... For where your treasure is, there your heart will be also" (Matthew 6:20, 21).

✤ What treasures are you chasing after?

✤ What treasures are you building?

✤ Are your treasures temporary, or will they last forever?

✤ How can you work toward finding treasures of the heart?

Some people work excessive overtime to pay off debts or meet financial goals. Others are so focused on making money that they become obsessed with doing so. At that point they begin to serve money instead of money serving them. Explain to your teen that by serving money, we become slaves. We need to use money as a tool and serve God instead!

 Remind your son or daughter that God is the true owner of all we possess and that when we share with and give to others, we're showing God our love ... and making *him* our master—not money!

It's possible that all this talk about the dangers of serving money may lead your teen to think that being wealthy is wrong. Not so. Throughout Scripture, God enabled individuals to accumulate vast amounts of wealth. The key is keeping *God* at the center of our hearts and not living to earn money. Have your teen identify at least two biblical figures who were wealthy. Analyze how they became wealthy and how they thanked God for their blessings. Then discuss what financial qualities should be embraced or avoided and why.

Teach your teen that a person's attitude toward finances is an indicator of his or her heart. Jesus said, "For where your treasure is, there your heart will be also" (Matthew 6:21). Jesus taught that what we do with money and possessions reflects what is in our hearts. As author Jim Burns put it: "Your heart will be devoted to the one you serve, and your actions will demonstrate which you are serving." Be sure your teen knows which is which!

Be grateful — not greedy.

We sing praise songs and read psalms of praise. But sometimes our thankfulness doesn't extend beyond expressions of the heart. When we are generous, we reach out to others less fortunate. That's one of the lessons gleaned from the parable of the good Samaritan (Luke 10:25-37). The good Samaritan had a heart to give and put his love into action by helping a stranger no one else would help. Sometimes God places us in churches, jobs, and even communities to help when no one else will. Seizing these opportunities helps us teach our teens to be generous.

> **key point**
> **A GIVING HEART REFLECTS CHRIST.**

> **key point**
> **AS YOU GIVE TO GOD, HE GIVES TO YOU.**

"Remember that the happiest people are not those getting more, but those giving more."

—H. Jackson Brown Jr.

When we teach teens to be generous, we prepare the way for God to use them. Indeed, your teen needs to understand that gratefulness is God's way. God's Word encourages gratitude and generosity while warning against greediness. Remind your son or daughter that, as Christians, we have the privilege of sharing with others while knowing that God will meet our own needs. Encourage memorizing verses such as Proverbs 11:25 and 22:9 to sidestep the temptation to be greedy instead of grateful.

Remind your teen that donating money means we cannot use it for personal gain. In other words, we may have to scratch something off of our must-have lists in order to lend a hand to someone else. Stimulate teens' generosity by matching giving with their interests. Teens may get excited about seasonal giving opportunities that enable them to help other teens. Or they may want to participate in fundraisers that benefit individuals who suffer from diseases that family members or friends have. By pinpointing such giving opportunities, we help teens experience the joy of giving.

key point
TITHING HONORS GOD WITH LOVE.

MIDDLE-SCHOOL MEMOS

Middle-school kids like making *Giving Banks*. Partition a small box into three compartments, then cut in the lid three slots: for saving, spending, and giving. Encourage your middle schooler to budget for each area regularly!

Tithing is one way to show our thanks for God's blessings. New and Old Testament verses encourage tithing, and even Jesus spoke about this practice. Training teens to tithe will be near impossible if we don't tithe ourselves. Explain to your teen that one of the easiest ways to tithe is by budgeting 10 percent of his income and giving it the church to help serve others. Remind your teen that God wants us to give out of cheerful, sacrificial hearts—not ones that begrudge giving!

More Americans claim to tithe than actually do: 17% of adults claim to tithe; 6% actually do so.

(Barna Group, 2000)

Investing in Tomorrow

Managing money wisely includes saving money regularly. When we get in the habit of saving a set amount each pay-check or month, we build a stronger financial future. Saving regularly, exercising patience, and resisting the urge to with-draw funds ensures that our savings grow from year to year.

Saving money secures our financial futures.

Where do you want to be financially in five, ten, or twenty years? How do you plan on getting there? If your plans do not include saving money, then you'll likely be disappointed, since saving assures we have enough money once we're ready to use it. Teaching teens to save helps them understand that saving money unlocks the door to financial security, while ushering them into other doors marked "Dreams Realized!"

Saving helps us reach goals.

It's actually easier than ever to save, thanks to the many savings options available. We can put money in a regular savings account, store it away in a certificate of deposit (CD), or invest in mutual funds and other investment products. We can establish tax-deferred 529 plans to help fund a college education. But despite the many options, our nation's savings rate recently dipped into the negative zone for the first time since the Great Depression! A negative rate reflects the fact that we're spending more than we're earning.

In the past 20 years, personal savings accounts have fallen dramatically! How can you help your teen develop healthy savings habits?

10.2%

2.8%

1980   2000

Saving money makes so much sense. It helps us reach goals and dreams. Instead of wishing for a new car or a college education, your teen can save money and *realize* her desires.

key point
LOST SAVINGS EQUAL LOST DREAMS!

key point
SAVINGS OPTIONS DO EXIST— USE THEM!

Saving is essential for emergencies and "rainy days." And teaching your teen to save helps prepare him for his future, including a first car, a first apartment, or even a wedding. The possibilities are endless!

Teens tend to live for today and don't recognize or anticipate future needs. Point out that security doesn't happen magically—it must be planned and provided for!

TRY THIS!

Take your teen on a virtual shopping trip. Shop for a car on the computer, then discuss how much time and money it would take to save for it. Discuss ways your teen can begin saving money for a first car, even if it's not the pricey one she's dreaming of.

Remind your teen that putting off saving today means having less money in the future. When teens start saving today, they have ample time to see accounts grow to meet both short- and long-term savings goals. Discuss how saving for big-ticket items is the best way to get them. Chat about how college becomes more affordable when teens save regularly. Remind your son or daughter that saving money isn't always easy, but it always makes great sense—and cents!

Investing helps us achieve dreams.

If saving money is a good idea, then investing is a great one! Investing helps us grow our money in ways that a regular savings account can't, especially since the interest rates on traditional savings accounts continue to remain low. Another benefit of investing is that we can't touch funds before a specified time without being penalized—and losing some of the money invested. That fact provides incentive not to withdraw funds, thus helping us to stick to our original investment goals. When we encourage teens to invest their money, they discover ways to grow it rather than to spend it.

key point
INVESTING SPEEDS ALONG SAVINGS.

Discuss how the saying "Good things come to those who wait" applies to saving and investing.

Impatience is a 'tween's middle name. Remind her that it takes time to build dreams through saving and investing!

If you invest in a 401K plan, have certificates of deposit, or invest in other ways, do you talk about it at home? Does your teen see you watching investment-oriented television shows or checking stock performance in the newspaper? Do you read books to learn more about investment basics? Any of these practices could stimulate teens' appetites for investing. As always, if we don't practice what we preach, teens will be less likely to follow our advice. If you haven't begun investing in even small ways, now's a good time to start!

Teens need to know that investing is usually a long-term approach to savings. It's not necessarily for people seeking to use funds in a couple of months, although six-month certificates of deposit (CDs) remain popular. Challenge your teen to look at investing as a way to build financial security. Get him excited about investing by encouraging him to research books and websites especially for teen investors or to chat with a financial advisor at your bank. Such resources help teens understand how investing money today can provide for a better tomorrow.

BIG BIBLE POINT

Read Mark 4:26-29 aloud with your teen and discuss:

• How is an investor like the man in the parable?

• Although you may not fully understand how investing works, why should we still consider investing?

• Why is it wise to put investing to work for your future?

5 WAYS TO INVEST!

certificates of Deposit

stock market

money-market funds

public utilities

bonds

Give teens a taste for what it is like to invest in several ways. Use online investing tutorials like those founds at www.msfinancialsavvy.com. These tutorials can help your teen learn investment basics, including picking stocks and building a portfolio based on interests and goals. Your teen may also catch the investment bug if you offer to put a certain amount of money in a CD or money-market fund based on his initial investment—perhaps one dollar for every $5 he invests. Another option might be to buy your teen one or more shares of stock in a company that he is familiar with. Special rules apply to giving stock as gifts, so make sure you talk to your financial advisor about those that apply to gifts to minors.

REMEMBER: Riskier investments pay bigger returns— but can cause bigger falls, too. Invest carefully for your future!

It's important to invest with interest.

A free offer can be a good one, especially when it comes to interest: the free money earned on our deposits. If you live by the adage that *a penny saved is a penny earned*, you can make your money work smarter, not harder, by saving with interest. Teach your teen to seek ways to grow his money by opting for interest-bearing accounts.

Simple savings accounts add up.

key point
INTEREST PAYS BIG DIVIDENDS!

Have you ever heard stories of people placing their savings under their mattresses or in shoeboxes? The goal is to have a safe, handy place to store savings. Well, these methods aren't the best, or safest, ways to protect funds, as theft or fire could easily wipe away hard-earned savings! Plus, there is no way for the savings to grow. The same holds true for storing money in a piggy bank!

Though piggy banks are interesting, they don't pay interest on your savings!

A TYPICAL SAVINGS ACCOUNT IN TODAY'S MARKET PAYS ABOUT 2 PERCENT INTEREST.

Passbook savings accounts make good sense. First, money is more secure, since the federal government insures deposits at banks or credit unions. Second, a passbook lists each deposit and withdrawl and must be brought to the bank for each transaction. The great thing about such simple accounts is that you usually can open one with very little cash—in some cases just a dollar! Another advantage is the earned interest on monies deposited.

Simple interest-bearing accounts usually offer a higher interest rate than a passbook account, but they may require a higher initial deposit or balance before earning interest. Both types of accounts allow for direct deposits of your teen's paychecks, making it easier to save. Since interest is like free money, it makes sense to open either account. Since most checking accounts pay little if any interest, encourage your teen to place extra money in his savings account.

TARGET MOMENT

Encourage teens to get cash for "trash." Hold a garage sale or donate used items to a nonprofit organization— and be sure to get a receipt for a tax write-off.

MARRIED PEOPLE LIST MONEY AND FINANCES AS THE SECOND BIGGEST CONCERN THEY FACE!

36% — CHILDREN AND FAMILY ISSUES

32% — MONEY AND FINANCES

19% — RELIGION AND BELIEFS

7% — WORK-RELATED ISSUES

5% — OTHER ISSUES

(*USA Today* and Findlaw.com)

A simple savings account is teen-friendly. Younger teens may especially appreciate passbook accounts because they get the pleasure of visiting the bank to make deposits and having a visual picture of their growing accounts. Older teens may appreciate the ease of depositing funds in an interest-bearing account and receiving statements. In either case, encourage your teen to save regularly with interest. Remind your teen that the longer funds are held, and the higher the balance, the more interest he or she stands to earn.

key point
DON'T STASH CASH AT HOME!

Stocks and bonds can be risky business.

Saving money holds such promise! We put funds aside to meet goals, help in emergencies, and secure our financial futures. These are some of the very same reasons for investing. Investing offers more choices and greater financial flexibility than putting extra funds aside in checking accounts or simple interest-bearing accounts.

key point
BE CAREFUL WHEN INVESTING MONEY!

✓**SAFETY**

✓**INCOME**

✓**GROWTH**

Three primary reasons to invest: to help us keep our money secure, increase our funds, and grow toward personal goals and dreams!

Explain to your teen about types of investments and their pluses and minuses. What we choose to invest in depends on our goals and available funds, but rates of return and inherent risks are factors to consider. Urge your teen to be conservative with his first experiences in investing.

INVEST IN COMMON SENSE WHEN CHOOSING INVESTMENTS!

❖ Government savings bonds, mutual funds, 401K plans, certificates of deposit, and Keogh accounts are investment options.

❖ Bonds are sold and backed by governments and utilities that pay us to borrow our money.

❖ Stocks are sold by companies, enabling us to own a small part of a company.

The whole concept of investing is based on "tomorrow"—be that a day, week, or longer. Sometimes it takes years for a specific investment to realize the kind of growth we long for. Remind your teen that investing comes with no guarantees, so we should never put all our eggs in one basket! Having several different types of investments adds balance and lowers risk. Help your teen nurture patience by discussing what the future would be like without money and how investing can help us plan better.

Encourage your teen to chat with financial officers at your bank or other investment firms to learn about types of investments, their risks, and possible returns.

BIG BIBLE POINT

Read Ecclesiastes 7:14 with your teen and discuss:

- How can investing make us prosperous?

- What could cause a "day of adversity" (i.e., stock market drop) in investing?

- How does the verse relate to the future and wisdom of saving and investing money?

Talk to risk-adverse teens about the benefits and pitfalls of investing. Then encourage them to invest anyway! Make a list of activities your teen or family engage in that entail some risk, such as driving a car, riding a bicycle, or flying in airplanes. Then discuss what your lives would be like without those activities and why the benefits far outweigh the risks. Use the discussion to stimulate further interest in investing. If possible, make an appointment with a family friend or church member who can shed more light on investing basics.

DID YOU KNOW...

Many organizations now offer free or low-cost workshops on various money matters for teens. With your teen, scan local newspapers for listings, then choose one to attend.

Compound interest compounds growth!

In Matthew 13 Jesus likens the kingdom of Heaven to a mustard seed, noting it is the smallest of seeds but has great growth potential. Like a mustard seed, our money can grow beyond expectations with compound interest. This is interest earned on interest—how cool is that! Explain to your son or daughter that when we invest or save money, we earn interest only on the principle amount of our investment—the amount we originally save or invest. Compound interest, on the other hand, is paid on *both* the principle and any earned interest we're due.

key point
MONEY CAN GROW LIKE MUSTARD SEEDS!

Take time to explain how simple and compound interest work. This is a confusing time for your teen as far as finances, but you'll reap big dividends later as your teen becomes a money-savvy adult!

Usually we think of compound interest as fees added to loans and credit cards that increase the money we owe. But for saving and investing purposes, compound interest works for, not against, us. The longer you invest, the greater the benefits of compound interest. If you invest $100 (your principle) at 10 percent interest compounded quarterly, at the end of five years you'll have $161. And that's not bad, since the $61 extra is really like getting free money. Compound interest adds up much faster than simple interest!

COMPOUND INTEREST IS THE GREAT MONEY MULTIPLIER!

CHAPTER 4 — INVESTING IN TOMORROW

key point

COMPOUND INTEREST MULTIPLIES MONEY!

Discuss with your teen the compound-interest chart below and point out how dramatically savings increase after several years. Try using a compound-interest calculator to help your teen see just how her savings can grow. Discuss how a CD or money-market fund may help secure your teen's financial future. Check out investment clubs for teens. Research with teens such clubs and whether one would be beneficial.

Remind your teen that the greater the principal amount and the longer he saves, the more money he'll make. That extra interest can make a difference in whether your teen is working when he's 75—or driving a cool sports car!

Remind your teen how God rewarded Abraham for his patience and obedience with great wealth!

INVESTING WITH COMPOUND INTEREST
Here's how a $100 investment would grow based on a 10% interest rate ...

Number of Years Invested	Simple Interest	Compound Interest
1 year	$110	$110
5 years	$150	$161
10 years	$200	$259
20 years	$300	$672
30 years	$400	$1,744
40 years	$500	$4,526

Lost time equals lost money.

Mark Twain quipped, "Never put off till tomorrow what you can do the day after tomorrow"—and some of us have taken this to heart! But procrastination results in lost time and money. Help teens understand that we maximize money management when we get an early start on saving and investing and consistently stick to financial goals.

Don't put off saving for tomorrow.

Ever notice how quickly tomorrow comes? We put aside certain tasks like cleaning, washing the car, or mowing the lawn in hopes that we'll have more time tomorrow—or that, at the least, we'll want to do these things the following day. Eventually we learn that putting most things off until tomorrow just makes our lives more difficult.

key point
DON'T DELAY SAVING OR INVESTING.

key point
MONEY IS TIED TO TIME.

Waiting until tomorrow makes our financial lives harder, too. By delaying or failing to save, we may find it more difficult to reach financial goals, especially those for which we need years to accumulate. Retirement is a good example. You may picture yourself retiring early and doing things you've dreamed of. But if you wait too long to begin saving, you may not reach those goals.

DISCUSSION STARTER

"Procrastination is opportunity's assassin."
—Victor Kiam

What does this quote mean in relation to saving money?

Teens need to understand that delay causes missed opportunities. Help your teen see this by sharing everyday events that reveal the power of procrastination—including saving money during sales and getting new jobs. When we delay using store or manufacturer's coupons, we miss saving money on things we want or need. When we delay sending out a resume or making a job interview after a prospective employer expresses interest in our skills, we miss the chance to get a new or better job. Procrastination hurts!

MIDDLE-SCHOOL MEMOS

Help your young teen understand the affects of procrastination by reading together a modern version of Aesop's "The Ant and the Grasshopper." Chat about how putting things off can hurt us in the long run, including how we save money for a "long winter."

Never put off till **tomorrow** what you can do today.
—Thomas Jefferson

You may never be a millionaire, but it's important to save and invest in order to be comfortable for the future—and for today!

Teens may not be totally convinced that waiting until tomorrow is a bad idea since they think they have decades of tomorrows ahead of them to accomplish goals. Despite such attitudes, challenge your teen to strike while the iron is hot for saving or investing. Ask him to seriously think about where he wants to be financially by age 25, 30, or 40. Then ask him to explain how he could reach those goals. Discuss how saving and investing today can affect his future tomorrow and in years to come.

THE **POWER** OF PROCRASTINATION . . . & **$**AVING

If you think it doesn't matter when you begin to save, think again! Check out this chart to see what the negative power of procrastination can mean to your financial future!

THE POWER OF PROCRASTINATION

Person A			Person B		
Age	Payment	Accumulation End of Year	Age	Payment	Accumulation End of Year
22	$2,000	$2,254	22	$0	$0
23	$2,000	$4,793	23	$0	$0
24	$2,000	$7,655	24	$0	$0
25	$2,000	$10,879	25	$0	$0
26	$2,000	$14,513	26	$0	$0
27	$2,000	$18,607	27	$0	$0
28	$0	$20,967	28	$2,000	$2,254
29	$0	$23,626	29	$2,000	$4,793
30	$0	$24,622	30	$2,000	$7,655
31	$0	$29,999	31	$2,000	$10,879
32	$0	$33,803	32	$2,000	$14,513
37	$0	$61,410	37	$2,000	$40,877
42	$0	$111,563	42	$2,000	$88,774
47	$0	$202,676	47	$2,000	$175,788
52	$0	$368,200	52	$2,000	$333,867
57	$0	$668,907	57	$2,000	$621,048
62	$0	$1,215,202	62	$2,000	$1,142,768
65	$0	$1,738,673	65	$2,000	$1,640,437

* based on a 12% IRA

$MART $AVINGS!

Rainy days and retirement are both in your teen's future. Will he or she be ready for them? This chart shows how saving consistently and regularly from young adulthood through the earning years can really add up!

IF YOU COULD SAVE $100 PER MONTH, JUST LOOK AT YOUR LONG-TERM SAVINGS!

Annual Percentage Rate	In 10 Years	In 15 Years	In 20 Years	In 25 Years	In 30 Years
8.0	$18,120.59	$34,215.46	$58,131.59	$93,669.69	$146,477.45
9.0	$19,135.85	$37,335.13	$65,737.27	$110,053.95	$179,213.66
10.0	$20,220.77	$40,797.48	$74,514.81	$129,964.60	$220,297.80

*compounded quarterly

"You can be young without money, but you can't be old without it." —Tennessee Williams

There's growth power in consistent savings!

key point
PATIENCE IS KEY IN SAVING FOR GOALS.

Some things never change—like get-rich-quick schemes that tempt us to throw away our goals and money in order to be prosperous. By the time you're involved in the scheme, you realize that personal goals are more out of reach than ever before. Teens are especially impatient and willing to take quick paths, but deals that are simply too fast and good to be true usually are! They promise much but deliver little. It's important to teach teens about having perseverance and patience because, although God can do the miraculous, most of our goals, including those related to finances, won't be realized overnight.

key point
DEALS THAT SOUND "TOO GOOD" USUALLY AREN'T!

Saving money requires more than cash—it also requires time … and the patience of a statue!

In fact, to secure the futures we're dreaming of, we'll need to save consistently, dollar by dollar, year by year. And we'll need to exercise the "three Ps" of saving: *planning, patience,* and *perseverance.* As we do, we'll begin to see our bank balances increase and investment accounts grow, while securing our financial futures. When we teach teens to do the same, they'll be able to embrace the words of the little engine that declared, "I think I can, I think I can," as they save more and spend less!

1. PLANNING

2. PATIENCE

3. PERSEVERANCE

Remember the tale of "The Tortoise and The Hare"? It's been years since you've read it to your child, but the story remains relevant to many areas of life, including money management. While the hare initially outran the tortoise, he lost the race. Why? His cocky attitude caused him to underestimate his competition, lose focus, and rest at a crucial point during the competition. Persevering despite obstacles is a key moral of this story.

Slow, sure, and consistent is the way to grow solid savings!

TRY THIS!
To show how something can grow, consider baking fresh bread using yeast to multiply and grow the dough. What a tasty way of showing how patience and growth are linked!

Like the tortoise, we need to persevere while saving money. Discuss with your teen how perseverance plays a role in money management. Try popping two bags of microwave popcorn, stopping one bag midway through the process while allowing the other its full course. Talk about the results and how patience (or the lack thereof) affected the quality and quantity of the kernels popped. Challenge your teen to list three financial goals: one for the next month, one for the next five years, and one for retirement age. Encourage your teen to read her goals often and work toward reaching them with patience, perseverance, and planning!

7 out of 10 teens haven't thought seriously about their future finances.

73%

"Let us run with perseverance the race marked out for us"
(Hebrews 12:1). Don't allow impatience to upset your goals!

Even the rich save and invest regularly!

Teens dream big! Encourage them to pursue their dreams of tomorrow by making wise money decisions today!

Who wants to be a millionaire? We all dream of being financially secure so that we needn't worry about every penny spent or saved. Yet even millionaires save. It's true! Although the affluent have hundreds and thousands of dollars more than most of us, they realize that money is a limited resource that must be used and saved wisely. Teaching teens that even the wealthy save money helps them realize that saving and investing are not just hobbies—they're a money-management *lifestyle*!

key point

EVEN MILLIONAIRES SAVE AND SPEND WITH CARE!

TRY THIS!

Challenge your teen to list what he would do with a million dollars. Would he invest it? If so, how? Would he purchase a house or cars and trips? Or would that money be used to serve others in amazing ways? Discuss the list and how people use money, once they have it, for both good or selfish purposes.

Stories about self-made millionaires are especially interesting and inspiring. One thread that runs through many of these stories is that what seemed like "overnight success" actually took years to accomplish while the spotlighted individuals worked hard and used the same "three Ps" of saving to secure their futures. Remind your teen of the power of planning, patience, and perseverance. If wealthy people didn't apply sound money-management techniques, they would not be millionaires.

Where God guides, God provides! Be a good steward of his blessings, no matter what your finances may be.

Stories also abound about individuals who lost fortunes through unwise living and wasteful spending! Some of your teen's favorite athletes and stars probably fit into this category. Talking with teens about the dangers of squandering earnings or failing to save brings home the point that God entrusts us with money and provides resources that are designed for today and tomorrow. Asking God's help to avoid money mistakes and handling money well by earning, spending, and saving wisely assures we'll meet most of our wants and needs—even if we never become millionaires.

BIG BIBLE POINT

Read aloud Ecclesiastes 7:11, 12 with your teen. Discuss the following questions.

- How is wisdom a valuable inheritance?

- How can wisdom be of more value than money?

- How does God provide for both security and wisdom?

REMEMBER:
A man is rich according to who he is—not what he has!

Teens growing up in a society where young people acquire wealth at an early age through career choices or entrepreneurship may actually say they want to be *billionaires*, or better. Don't squash such dreams, because anyone could become a millionaire. Instead, work toward such dreams and help your teen do the same. Challenge him to handle money wisely, encourage him to save and invest consistently, and remind him that God expects us to share with others!

BUDGET SHEET	AMOUNT OF MONEY
INCOME	
FROM JOB	$
FROM ALLOWANCE	$
OTHER	$
EXPENSES	
MEALS & SNACKS	$
CAR PAYMENT	$
INSURANCE	$
CLOTHING	$
SCHOOL SUPPLIES	$
ENTERTAINMENT	$
HEALTH (doctor, dentist)	$
SPENDING MONEY	
SAVINGS/INVESTMENTS	
	$
DONATIONS	
	$

REMEMBER: YOUR SAVINGS, EXPENSES, AND DONATIONS SHOULD
EQUAL YOUR INCOME. IF YOU HAVE EXTRA—SAVE EVEN MORE!

MONEY ACTIVITY CHART

DATE	FOR	DEPOSIT +	WITH-DRAWAL −	INTEREST	BALANCE

REMEMBER: LOG IN ALL OF YOUR DEPOSITS AND WITHDRAWALS!
CHECK BANK STATEMENTS FOR INTEREST AMOUNTS.

More Resources

BOOKS

for teens

- David Gardner, Tom Gardner, and Selena Maranjian, *The Motley Fool Investment Guide for Teens* (Simon & Schuster, 2002).
- Robert T. Kiyosaki, *Rich Dad, Poor Dad for Teens: The Secrets About Money That You Don't Learn in School* (Warner Books, 2004).
- Susan Shelly, *The Complete Idiot's Guide to Money for Teens* (Alpha, 2001).
- Michael Stahl, *Early to Rise: A Young Adult's Guide to Investing ... and Financial Decisions That Can Shape Your Life* (expanded edition, Silver Lake Publishing, 2005).
- Keltie Thomas, *The Kids Guide to Money Cents* (Kids Can Press, 2004).

for parents

- Mary Hunt, *Debt-Proof Your Marriage* (Fleming H. Revell, 2003).
- Ellie Kay, *A Woman's Guide to Family Finances* (Bethany House, 2005).
- Karen O'Connor, *Addicted to Shopping ... and Other Issues Women Have With Money* (Harvest House, 2005).
- Cynthia Sumner, *Dollars and Sense: A Mom's Guide to Money Matters* (MOPS International, 2005).
- Michelle Singletary, *Seven Money Mantras for a Richer Life: How to Live Well With the Money You Have* (Random House, 2004).

WEBSITES

- www.bankrate.com (financial news, planning tips, investment calculators, and much more).
- www.younginvestor.com/teens (a teen-friendly site giving the scoop on what investing is all about).
- www.jumpstart.org (the official site of the Jump$tart Coalition for Personal Financial Literacy).
- www.learntosave.com (information, activities, piggy banks, and more).
- www.ntrbonline.org (the teen portion of the National Endowment for Financial Education website).
- www.publicdebt.treas.gov/sav/savkids.htm (an online guide to savings bonds for kids).
- www.sba.gov/teens (the U.S. Small Business Administration's guide for teens wanting to start their own business).

GAMES

- *Money Matters* (Larry Burkett/Crown Financial).

Subpoint Index

Chapter 3: Spending & Serving Today   54

Chapter 4: Investing in Tomorrow   72